English
Picture Dictionary

English

Picture Dictionary

Berlitz Publishing/APA Publications GmbH & Co. Verlag KG
Singapore Branch, Singapore

Contacting the Editors
Every effort has been made to provide accurate information in this publication, but changes are inevitable. The publisher cannot be responsible for any resulting loss, inconvenience or injury. We would appreciate it if readers would call our attention to any errors or outdated information by contacting Berlitz Publishing, 95 Progress Street, Union, NJ 07083, USA.
Fax: 1-908-206-1103, email: comments@berlitzbooks.com

Cover illustration by Chris L. Demarest
Interior illustrations by Chris L. Demarest (pages 3, 5, 7-9, 12-23, 26-43, 46-51, 54-67, 70-75, 78-85, 88-107, and 110-119)
Anna DiVito (pages 24, 25, 52, 53, 76, 77, 86, 87, and 120-123)
Claude Martinot (pages 10, 11, 44, 45, 68, 69, 108, and 109)

Printed in Singapore by Insight Print Services (Pte) Ltd.,March 2005

Dear Parents,

The Berlitz Kids™ *Picture Dictionary* will create hours of fun and productive learning for you and your child. Children love sharing books with adults, and reading together is a natural way for your child to develop language skills in an enjoyable and entertaining way.

In 1878, Professor Maximilian Berlitz had a revolutionary idea about making language learning accessible and fun. These same principles are still successfully at work today. Now, more than a century later, research shows that children learn their first language just like they learn a foreign language—through instruction and interaction with teachers, parents or caregivers. Berlitz Kids™ combines the time-honoured traditions of Professor Berlitz with this current research to create superior products that truly help children learn any language.

Berlitz Kids™ materials let your child gain access to language in a positive way. The content and vocabulary in this book have been carefully chosen by language experts to provide basic words and phrases that form the foundation of a core vocabulary. In addition, the book will delight your child, since each word is used in an amusing sentence, and then illustrated in an engaging style. The pictures are a great way to capture your child's attention!

You will notice that most words are listed as separate entries. Every so often, though, there is a special page that shows words grouped together by theme. For example, if your child is especially interested in animals, he or she will find a special Animals page with lots of words and pictures grouped there. In addition, to help your child with phrases used in basic conversation, you and your child may want to look at the back of the book, where phrases about such things as meeting new people and a family dinner can be found.

The Berlitz Kids™ *Picture Dictionary* has an easy-to-use index at the back of the book. This index lists the words in alphabetical order, and gives the page number where the word appears in the main part of the book.

We hope the Berlitz Kids™ *Picture Dictionary* will provide you and your child with hours of enjoyable learning.

The Editors at Berlitz Kids™

a/an

A sandwich and an apple are the cat's lunch.

across

The fork is across from the spoon.

add

I like to add numbers.

adventure

What an adventure!

aeroplane

See Transportation (page 108).

afraid

The elephant is afraid.

after

She eats an apple after lunch.

again

She jumps again and again.

agree

They need to agree.

air

A balloon is full of air.

airport

Aeroplanes land at an airport.

all

All the frogs are green.

alligator

See Animals (page 10).

almost

He can almost reach it.

along

There are birds along the path.

already

He already has a hat.

and

I have two sisters and two brothers.

answer

Who wants to answer the teacher's question?

A

ant

See Insects (page 53).

apple

The apple is falling.

April

The month after March is April.

arm

See People (page 76).

armadillo

Some armadillos live in Mexico.

around

Someone is walking around the stool.

art

Is it art?

as

He is as tall as a tree!

Animals

kangaroo
monkey
elephant
lion
giraffe
bear
jaguar
llama
alligator
snake
hippopotamus
fox

cow

horse

cock

goat

rabbit

sheep

hen

pig

fish

duck

frog

A

ask

It is time to ask, "Where are my sheep?"

at

The cat is at home.

attic

See Rooms in a House (page 86).

August

The month after July is August.

aunt

My aunt is my mum's sister.

autumn

Leaves fall in autumn.

awake

The duck is awake.

away

The cat is going away.

baby

The baby likes
to eat bananas.

back

She is
scratching
his back.

backyard

There is a
dinosaur in
our backyard!

bad

What a bad,
bad monster!

bag

The bag is full.

bakery

Mmm!
Everything at
the bakery
smells great!

ball

Can he
catch the ball?

balloon

It is a balloon!

banana

The bananas
are in the bowl.

band

The band
plays loudly.

bandage

She has a bandage on her knee.

bank

Put your money into the bank!

bark

Dogs like to bark.

baseball

See Games and Sports (page 44).

basement

See Rooms in a House (page 87).

basket

What is in the basket?

basketball

See Games and Sports (page 44).

bat

The bat is sleeping.

bat

Hit the ball with the baseball bat!

bath

She is in the bath.

bathroom

See Rooms in a House (page 86).

be

Would you like to be my friend?

beach

I like to play at the beach.

beans

He likes to eat beans.

bear

See Animals (page 10).

beautiful

Look at the beautiful flowers!

because

She is wet because it is raining.

bed

The bed is next to the table.

bedroom

See Rooms in a House (page 86).

bee

See Insects (page 53).

beetle

See Insects (page 52).

before

Put on your socks before you put on your shoes.

begin

She begins to paint.

behind

The boy is
behind the tree.

believe

This is too good
to believe.

bell

Don't ring that bell!

belt

See Clothing (page 24).

berry

Those berries
look good.

best

The red box
is the best.

better

The belt is
better than
the pin.

between

He is between
two trees.

bicycle

See Transportation (page 108).

big

He is very big.

bird

The bird is flying south for the winter.

birthday

She is one year old today. Happy birthday!

biscuit

Mary wants a biscuit.

black

See Numbers and Colours (page 69).

blank

The pages are blank.

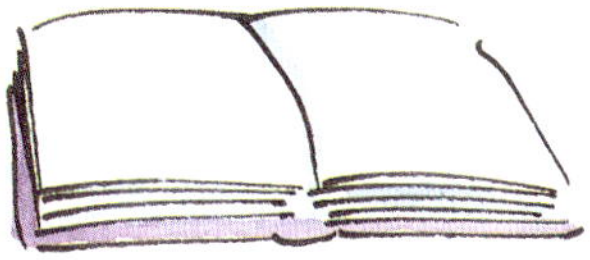

blanket

What is under that blanket?

blouse

See Clothing (page 25).

blow

The wind is starting to blow.

blue

See Numbers and Colours (page 69).

boat

See Transportation (page 109).

book

I am reading a book.

bookshop

You can buy a book at a bookshop.

boots

See Clothing (page 25).

bottle

The straw is in the bottle.

bowl

Some food is still in the bowl.

bowling

See Games and Sports (page 44).

box

Why is that fox in the box?

boy

The boys are brothers.

branch

Oh, no! Get off that branch!

brave

What a brave mouse!

bread

He likes bread with jam and butter.

break

It is easy to break an egg.

breakfast

Morning is the time for breakfast.

bridge

The boat is under the bridge.

bring

She wants to bring the lamb to school.

broom

A broom is for sweeping.

brother

He is my brother.

brown

See Numbers and Colours (page 69).

brush

I need my brush.

bubble

The bath is full of bubbles.

bug

Do you know the name of this bug?

build

I want to build a box.

bus

See Transportation (page 109).

bush

There is a bird in the bush.

busy

He is very busy.

but

The pencil is on the table, but the book is on the chair.

butter

The bread and butter taste good.

butterfly

See Insects (page 52).

button

One button is missing.

buy

He wants to buy a banana.

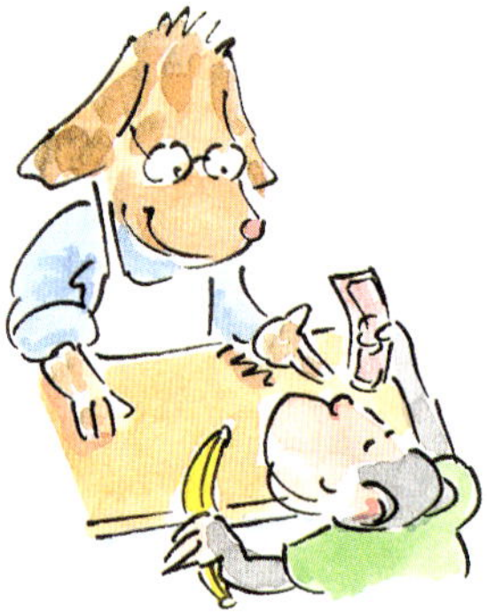

by

She is standing by the cheese.

cage

The bird is on the cage.

cake

She likes to eat cake.

call

Remember to call me again.

camel

The camel is hot.

camera

Smile at the camera!

can

What is in that can?

candle

She is lighting the candle.

cap

See Clothing (page 24).

car

See Transportation (page 109).

card

I have five cards.

cardigan

See Clothing (page 25).

care

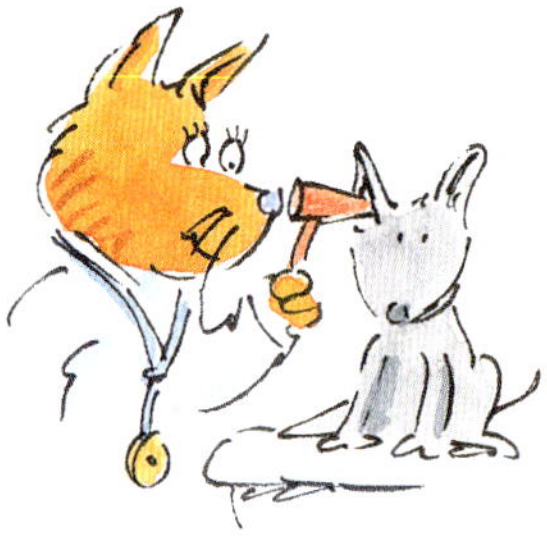

Her job is to care for pets.

carpenter

A carpenter makes things with wood.

carrot

A carrot is orange.

carry

Are you sure you want to carry that?

castanet

Click the castanets to the music!

castle

The king lives in a castle.

cat

The cat sees the mouse.

catch

He runs to catch the ball.

caterpillar

See Insects (page 53).

cave

Who lives in the cave?

celebrate

They are here to celebrate his birthday.

chair

He is sitting on a chair.

chalk

You can use chalk to write.

change

He wants to change his shirt.

cheer

It is fun to cheer for our team.

cheese

The mouse likes to eat cheese.

Clothing

jumper
waistcoat
hat
raincoat
cap
earmuffs
shirt
tie
jacket
belt
trousers
gloves
socks

trainers
dress
coat
mittens
scarf
blouse
boots
cardigan
skirt
shoes
shawl

cherry

He wants
a cherry.

child

She is a
happy child.

chocolate

He likes
chocolate.

circle

The robot is
drawing a circle.

circus

There are
clowns at
a circus.

city

This cow does
not live in
the city.

clap

He likes to
clap when he
is happy.

class

There is an
elephant
in my class.

classroom

A teacher works in a classroom.

clean (adjective)

The car is very clean.

clean (verb)

He cleans his room.

climb

The bear likes to climb the tree.

clock

A clock tells the time.

close (adverb)

The turtle is close to the rock.

close (verb)

He closes the window.

cloud

The sun is behind the cloud.

clown
The clown is funny.

coat
See Clothing (page 25).

cock
See Animals (page 11).

cold
It is cold in here!

comb (noun)
Where is
my comb?

comb (verb)
He combs
his hair.

come
Come here!

computer
She is working
at her computer.

cook
It is fun
to cook.

count
There are too
many stars
to count.

country

The country is beautiful.

cow

See Animals (page 11).

crayon

She is drawing with her crayons.

cricket

See Insects (page 53).

crowded

This lift is crowded.

cry

Don't cry!

cup

He is drinking water from the cup.

cupboard

See Rooms in a House (page 87).

cut

He cuts the carrots.

cute

She thinks her baby is cute.

cycling

See Games and Sports (page 45).

D

dad
My dad and
I look alike.

dance
The pig likes
to dance and
play the drum.

danger
He is in danger.

dark
It is dark
at night.

day
The sun shines
during the day.

December
The month
after November
is December.

decide
It is hard
to decide.

decision
That is a good
decision.

decoration
The decorations
look great!

deer

The deer is running in the woods.

dentist

The dentist has a big job.

department

This is the hat department.

desk

The desk is very messy.

different

The one in the middle is different.

difficult

This is difficult!

dig

A dog uses its paws to dig.

dining room

See Rooms in a House (page 86).

dinner

We eat dinner at six o'clock.

dinosaur

The dinosaur is having fun.

dirty

The pig is dirty.

dish

Do not drop the dishes!

do

He has a lot to do.

doctor

The doctor checks the baby.

dog

The dog has a funny hat.

doll

The doll is in the box.

dolphin

Dolphins live in the sea.

donkey

The donkey is sleeping.

door

What is behind the door?

down

The lift is going down.

dragon

The dragon is cooking lunch.

draw

He likes to draw.

drawing

Look at my drawing!

dress

See Clothing (page 25).

drink

She likes to drink milk.

drive

He is too small to drive.

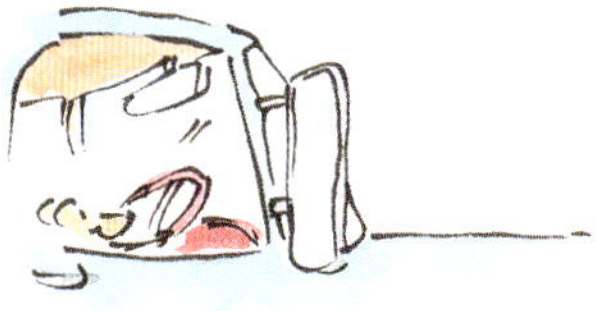

drop

He is going to drop the pie.

drum

He can play the drum.

dry

The tee shirt is dry.

duck

See Animals (page 11).

dust

There is dust under the bed.

E

each

Each snowflake
is different.

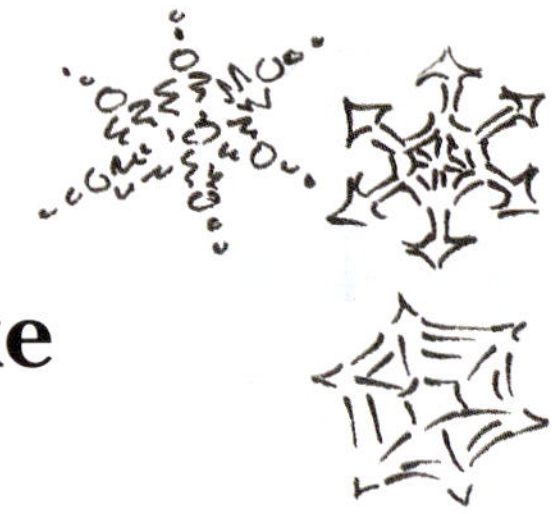

ear

See People (page 77).

early

The sun comes
up early.

earmuffs

See Clothing (page 24).

earn

We work to
earn money.

east

The sun rises
in the east.

eat

This bird likes
to eat worms.

egg

The hen laid
an egg.

eight

See Numbers and Colours (page 68).

eighteen

See Numbers and Colours (page 68).

eighty

See Numbers and Colours (page 69).

elephant

See Animals (page 10).

eleven

See Numbers and Colours (page 68).

empty

The bottle is empty.

E

end

It is time to end the game.

enough

He has enough food!

every

Every egg is cracked.

everyone

Everyone here has spots!

everything

Everything is purple.

everywhere

There are balls everywhere.

excited

He is excited.

eye

See People (page 76).

F

face

See People (page 76).

factory

Cans are made in this factory.

fall

He is about to fall.

family

This is a big family.

fan

Please turn off the fan!

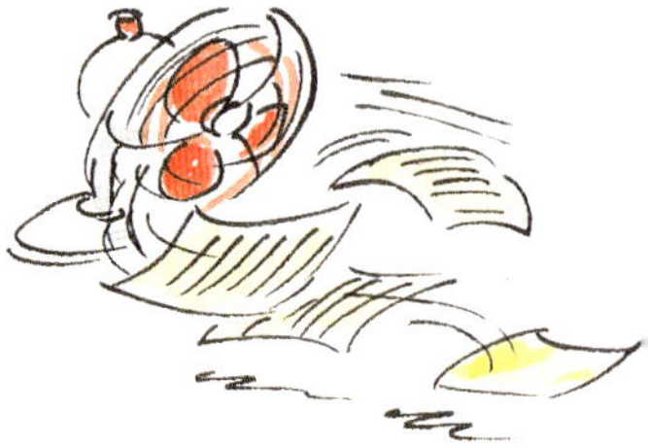

far

The moon is far away.

faraway

She is going to a faraway place.

fast

That train is going fast!

fat

The pig is fat.

father

My father and I look alike.

favourite

This is my favourite toy.

feather

The feather is tickling her nose.

February

The month after January is February.

feel

He likes to feel safe.

fence

There is a zebra on my fence.

fifteen

See Numbers and Colours (page 68).

fifty

See Numbers and Colours (page 69).

find

He is trying to find his kite.

finger

See People (page 76).

fire

He can put out the fire.

firefighter

The firefighter wears boots and a helmet.

firefly

See Insects (page 53).

fire station

Welcome to the fire station!

first

The yellow one is first in line.

fish

See Animals (page 11).

five

See Numbers and Colours (page 68).

fix

She wants to fix it.

flag

She is waving a flag.

flat (noun)

He is in the flat.

flat (adjective)

The tyre is flat.

flea

See Insects (page 52).

floor

There is a hole in the floor.

flower

The flower is growing.

flute

Robert plays the flute.

fly (noun)

See Insects (page 52).

fly (verb)

The bee cannot fly.

fog

He is walking in the fog.

food

He eats a lot of food.

foot

See People (page 76).

football

See Games and Sports (page 45).

for

This is for you.

forget

He does not want to forget his lunch!

fork

He eats with a fork.

forty
See Numbers and Colours (page 69).

four
See Numbers and Colours (page 68).

fourteen
See Numbers and Colours (page 68).

fox
See Animals (page 10).

Friday
On Friday, we go to the park.

fridge
We keep our snowballs in the fridge.

friend
He is my best friend.

frog
See Animals (page 11).

front
She sits in front of him.

fruit
He loves to eat fruit.

full
The cart is full of lizards.

fun
She is having fun.

funny
What a funny face!

game

Draughts is a game we play in the park.

garage

See Rooms in a House (page 86).

garden

Roses are growing in the garden.

gate

The gate is open.

get

The mice are trying to get the cheese.

giraffe

See Animals (page 10).

girl

The girl is dancing.

give

I want to give you a present.

glad

She is glad to see you.

glass

Windows are made of glass.

glasses

This owl wears glasses.

gloves

See Clothing (page 24).

go

Go to your room!

goat

See Animals (page 11).

golf

See Games and Sports (page 44).

good

What a good dog!

good-bye

Good-bye!

goose

A goose is riding a bicycle.

gorilla

The gorilla is eating a banana.

grab

She wants to grab the bananas.

grandfather

I have fun with my grandfather.

grandma

Grandma is my dad's mother.

grandmother

My grandmother likes to bake.

grandpa

Grandpa is my mum's father.

grape

The mouse likes to eat grapes.

grass

Cows eat grass.

grasshopper

See Insects (page 53).

Games and Sports

ice skating

football

skiing

tennis

cycling

swimming

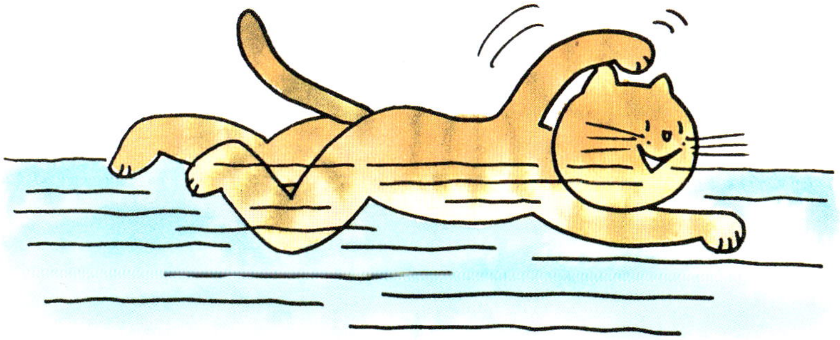

great

This is a great party.

green

See Numbers and Colours (page 69).

grey

See Numbers and Colours (page 69).

groceries

The groceries are falling out.

ground

They live in the ground.

group

This is a group of artists.

grow

He wants to grow.

guess

It is fun to guess what is inside.

guitar

My robot plays the guitar.

hair

See People (page 76).

hairdresser

The hairdresser cuts my hair.

half

Half the biscuit is gone.

hall

See Rooms in a House (page 87).

hammer

Hit the nail with the hammer!

hammock

Dad is sleeping in the hammock.

hand

See People (page 76).

happy

This is a happy face.

hard

The rock is hard.

harp

She plays the harp very well.

hat

See Clothing (page 24).

have

Soon they will all have hats.

he

He is under the table.

head

See People (page 76).

hear

See People (page 77).

heart

The heart is red.

helicopter

See Transportation (page 109).

hello

Hello.
How are you?

help

I need help!

hen

See Animals (page 11).

her/his

This is her tail.

here

I live here.

hi

Hi!

hide

She is too big to hide under the box.

high

The star is high in the sky.

hill

She is coming down the hill.

hippopotamus

See Animals (page 10).

hit

He hits
the ball.

hold

He has to hold
her hand now.

hole

He is digging
a hole.

holiday

They are
on holiday.

hooray

We are winning!
Hooray

hop

They know how
to hop.

horse

See Animals (page 11) and Transportation (page 109).

hospital

Doctors work at
the hospital.

hot

Fire is hot.

hotel

He is staying at
the hotel.

hour

In an hour, it is going to be two o'clock.

house

The house has many windows.

how

How does he do that?

hug

Give me a hug!

huge

That cat is huge!

hundred

See Numbers and Colors (page 68).

hungry

I think he is hungry.

hurry

She has to hurry.

hurt

It does not have to hurt.

husband

He is her husband.

I

"I am so cute!" she says.

ice

We skate on the ice.

ice cream

Clara likes ice cream.

idea

She has an idea.

important

He looks very important.

in

What is in that box?

inside

He is inside the house.

into

Do not go into that cave!

island

The goat is on an island.

Insects

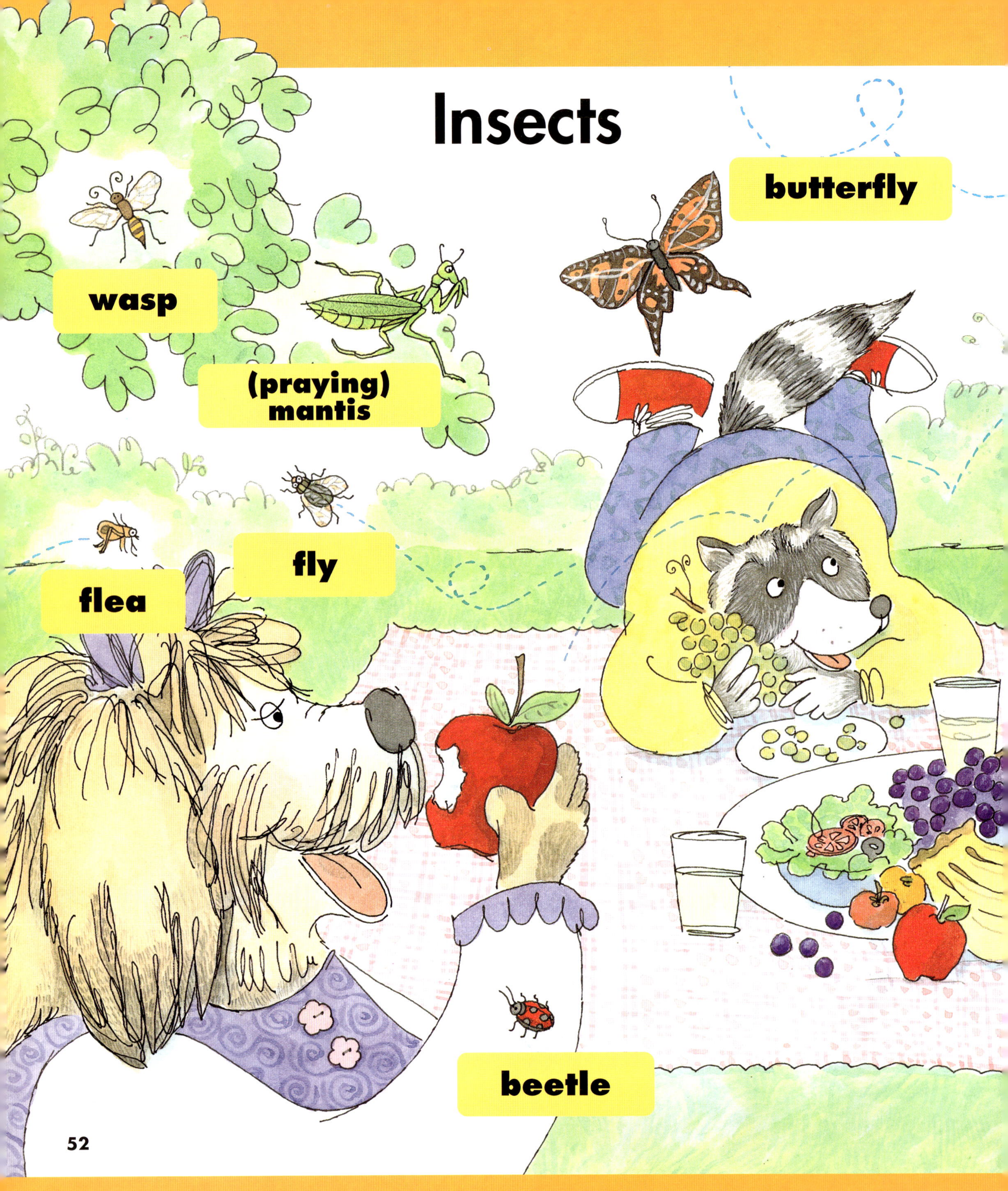

mosquito
caterpillar
grasshopper
moth
bee
termite
firefly
cricket
ant

J

jacket

See Clothing (page 24).

jaguar

See Animals (page 10).

jam

Do you think she likes bread and jam?

January

January is the first month of the year.

jar

Jam comes in a jar.

job

It is a big job.

juice

She is pouring a glass of orange juice.

July

The month after June is July.

jump

The animal loves to jump.

jumper

See Clothing (page 24).

June

The month after May is June.

junk

No one can use this junk.

kangaroo
See Animals (page 10).

keep
He wants to keep the dog.

key
Which key opens the lock?

kick
He wants to kick the ball.

kind (adjective)
She is kind to animals.

kind (noun)
What kind of animal is that?

king
The king is having fun.

kiss
Would you like to give the monkey a kiss?

kitchen

See Rooms in a House (page 86).

knife

A knife can cut things.

kite

Kites can fly high.

knock

He starts to knock on the door.

kitten

A kitten is a baby cat.

know

He wants to know what it says.

knee

See People (page 76).

ladder

He climbs the ladder.

lake

He is drinking from the lake!

lamp

He has a lamp on his head.

lap

He sits on his grandma's lap.

last

The pink one is last in line.

late

It is late at night.

laugh

It is fun to laugh.

lazy

He is so lazy.

leaf

The tree has one leaf.

leave

She does not want to leave.

left

This is your left hand.

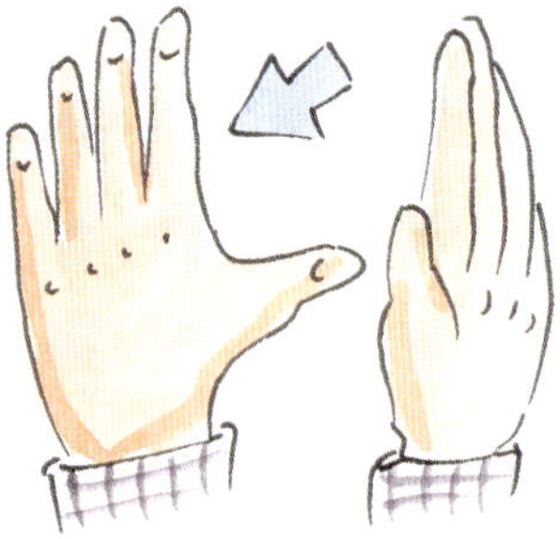

leg

See People (page 76).

lemon

She likes lemons.

leopard

One leopard is losing its spots.

let

Daddy is not going to let him go.

letter

This letter is going by airmail.

library

The library is full of books.

lick

Lick the ice cream before it melts!

life

Life is wonderful!

light

The sun gives us light.

lightning

Look! There's lightning!

like

He is going to like the cake.

like

She looks like a rock.

line

I can draw a line.

lion

See Animals (page 10).

listen

He does not want to listen to loud music.

little

The bug is little.

live

What a nice place to live!

living room

See Rooms in a House (page 87).

llama

See Animals (page 10).

lock

Do not forget to lock the door.

long

That is a long snake.

look

I use this to look at the stars.

lorry

See Transportation (page 109).

lose

He does not want to lose his hat.

lost

Oh, no!
He is lost.

lots

There are lots of bubbles.

loud

The music is loud!

love (verb)

She loves the present.

love (noun)

Love is wonderful.

low

The bridge is low.

lunch

He eats nuts for lunch.

mad

The frogs are mad at each other.

make

A belt is easy to make.

man

The man is waving.

mango

Is he going to eat the whole mango?

(praying) mantis

See Insects (page 52).

many

There are too many dots!

map

The map shows where to go.

maraca

Shake those maracas!

March

The month after February is March.

maths

He is not very good at maths.

May

The month after April is May.

maybe

Maybe it is a ball.

mayor

The mayor leads the town.

me

Look at me!

mean

That has to mean “hello”.

meat

I am eating meat, salad, and potatoes for dinner.

medicine

Take your medicine!

meet

It's a pleasure to meet you.

meow

Cats say, "MEOW!"

mess

What a mess!

messy

The bear is a little messy.

milk

He likes milk.

minute

It is one minute before noon.

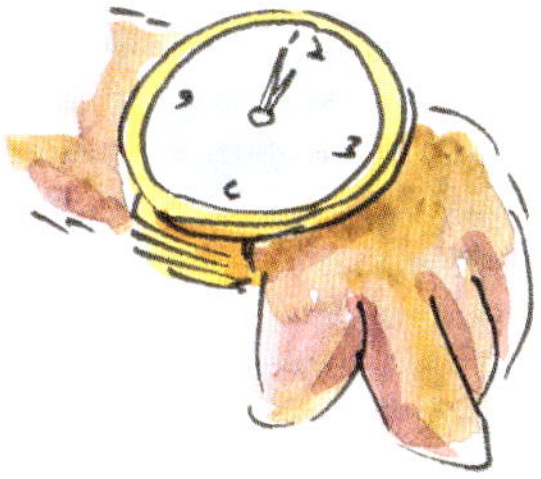

mirror

He loves to look in the mirror.

miss

He does not want to miss the aeroplane.

mittens

See Clothing (page 25).

mix

Use the spoon to mix it.

Monday

On Monday, we take baths.

money

Look at all the money!

monkey

See Animals (page 10).

month

January and February are the first two months of the year.

moon

The moon is up in the sky.

more

She needs to buy more juice.

morning

The sun comes up in the morning.

mosquito

See Insects (page 53).

most

Most of the milk is gone.

moth

See Insects (page 53).

mother

She is the baby's mother.

mountain

He is climbing up the mountain.

mouse

The mouse is skating.

mouth

See People (page 77).

move

They have to move.

movie

They are watching a movie.

Mr.

Say hello to Mr. Green.

Mrs.

Mrs. English is getting on the bus.

much

There is not much in the fridge.

mum

She is the baby's mum.

music

They can play music.

my

This is my nose.

N

nail

Try to hit the nail!

name

His name begins with “R”.

neck

See People (page 76).

necklace

She loves her necklace.

need

He is going to need a snack later.

neighbour

They are neighbours.

nest

The birds are near their nest.

never

She is never going to fly.

new

He has a new umbrella.

newspaper

Who cut my newspaper?

next (to)

She is next to the rock.

next

The horse is next.

nice

What a nice clown!

night

It is dark at night.

nine

See Numbers and Colours (page 68).

nineteen

See Numbers and Colours (page 68).

ninety

See Numbers and Colours (page 69).

no

No, you may not go.

noise

He is making a terrible noise.

noisy

They are very noisy.

noon

It is noon.

Numbers and Colours

0 nought **1** one **2** two **3** three **4** four **5** five **6** six

7 seven **8** eight **9** nine **10** ten **11** eleven **12** twelve

13 thirteen **14** fourteen **15** fifteen **16** sixteen

17 seventeen **18** eighteen **19** nineteen **20** twenty

30 **thirty**

40 **forty**

50 **fifty**

60 **sixty**

70 **seventy**

80 **eighty**

90 **ninety**

100 **one hundred**

1000 **one thousand**

Colours

grey

purple

yellow

black

green

red

blue

orange

tan

brown

pink

white

north

It is cold in the north.

nose

See People (page 77).

not

The bird is not red.

note

He is writing a note.

nothing

There is nothing in the bottle.

nought

See Numbers and Colours (page 68).

November

The month after October is November.

now

The mouse needs to run now.

number

There are five numbers.

nurse

She wants to be a nurse.

nut

I think he likes nuts.

ocean

This turtle swims in the ocean.

(one) o'clock

It is one o'clock.

October

The month after September is October.

of

The colour of the aeroplane is yellow.

oh

Oh! What a surprise!

old

The alligator is very old.

on

The coat is on the chair.

once

Birthdays come once a year.

one

See Numbers and Colours (page 68).

onion

He is chopping an onion.

only

This is the only food left.

open

The window is open.

or

Do you want the red one or the blue one?

orange

See Numbers and Colours (page 69).

orange

He is squeezing oranges.

ostrich

An ostrich can run fast.

other

What is on the other side?

ouch

Ouch! That hurts!

out

He is going out of the house.

outdoors

We like to play outdoors.

oven

We bake biscuits in the oven.

over

She is holding the umbrella over her head.

owl

The owl does not sleep at night.

own

He owns a book.

P

page
He is turning the page.

paint
The baby is sitting between the green and the blue paint.

painter
He is a painter.

pan
We cook in a pan.

panda
This panda is hungry.

paper
Write on the paper!

parent
These parents have many babies.

park
We like to go to the park.

parrot

This parrot can say, “Cracker!”

part

A wheel is part of the car.

party

The ants are having a party.

pat

The baby tries to pat the dog.

patio

See Rooms in a House (page 86).

pavement

They are playing on the pavement.

paw

He wants to shake paws.

pea

He does not like to eat peas.

peach

Peaches grow on trees.

pen

The pen is leaking.

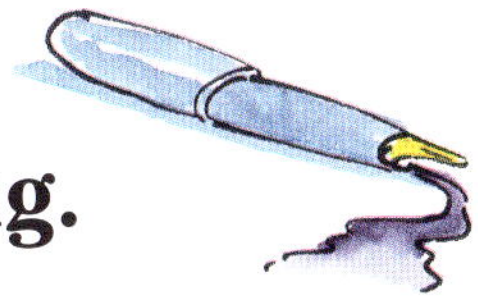

pencil

A pencil is used for drawing.

People • Your Body

ear
tooth
see
nose
touch
mouth
toe
hear
smell
taste

P

penguin

There is a penguin in the sink.

people

These people are going up.

pepper

She is using too much pepper.

peppers

Fresh peppers are tasty.

perfume

She is wearing perfume.

pet

This pig is a pet.

photograph

Look at the photograph!

piano

He plays the piano very well.

pick

This dog likes to pick berries.

picnic

They are having a picnic.

picture
This is a picture of a rabbit.

pie
Who is eating the pie?

pig
See Animals (page 11).

pillow
You sleep with your head on a pillow.

pink
See Numbers and Colours (page 69)

pizza
We like to eat pizza.

place
The doctor places the glasses on his nose.

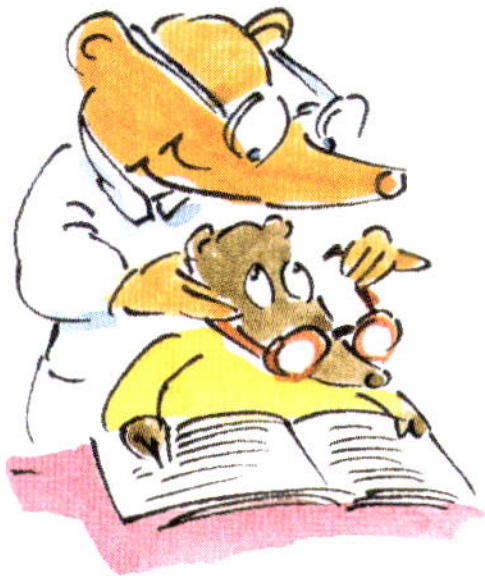

plan
It helps to plan ahead.

plant
He likes to plant nuts.

play
Do you want to play with us?

playground

Meet me at the playground!

playroom

See Rooms in a House (page 86).

please

Please feed me!

pocket

What is in his pocket?

point (noun)

It has a sharp point. Ouch!

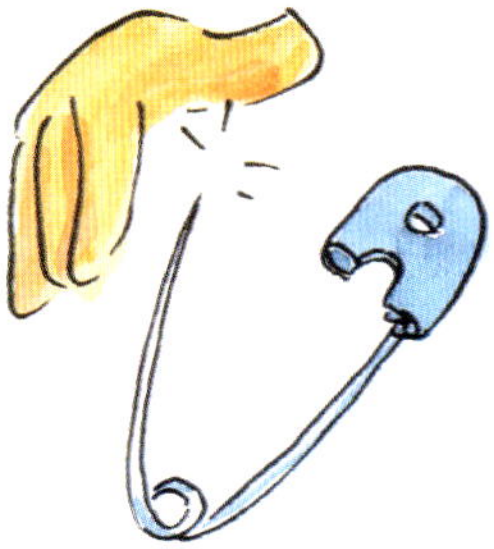

point (verb)

He points his finger at the duck.

policeman

The policeman helps us cross the street.

police station

You can get help at the police station.

polite

He is so polite!

pond

She falls into the pond.

poor

This poor monkey does not have much money.

porch

See Rooms in a House (page 87).

post

The post is here.

postbox

What is in that postbox?

postman

Our postman brings us the post.

post office

Letters go to the post office.

pot

It is time to stir the pot.

potato

These potatoes have eyes.

pound

Use a hammer to pound a nail.

present

Is the present for me?

pretty

It is not a pretty face.

prince

The prince is with his father.

princess

This princess has big feet.

prize

Look who wins the prize.

proud

She is proud of her new hat.

pull

We're trying to pull him up.

puppy

The puppy is wet.

purple

See Numbers and Colours (page 69).

purse

The purse is full.

push

He needs to push hard.

put

Don't put your foot in your mouth!

puzzle

Can you put the puzzle together?

pyjamas

She is wearing pyjamas to sleep.

quack

"Quack, quack, quack!" sing the ducks.

quarrel

We do not like to quarrel.

quarter

A quarter of the pie is gone.

queen

She is queen of the zebras.

question

She wants to ask a question.

quick

A rabbit is quick; a tortoise is slow.

quiet

Shh!
Be quiet!

quilt

Who is under the quilt?

quit

The raccoon wants to quit practicing.

quite

It is quite cold today.

R

rabbit
See Animals (page 11).

race

Who is going to win the race?

radio

They listen to the radio.

rain

She likes the rain.

rainbow

She is standing under a rainbow.

raincoat
See Clothing (page 24).

raindrop

Look at the raindrops.

raining

He is wet because it is raining.

read

Does he know how to read?

ready

The baby is not ready to go.

real

It is not a real dog.

really

She is really tall!

red

See Numbers and Colours (page 69).

remember

It is hard to remember his phone number.

restaurant

She is eating at a restaurant.

rice

Where is all the rice?

rich

He is very rich.

ride

It is fun to ride a horse.

right

This is your right hand.

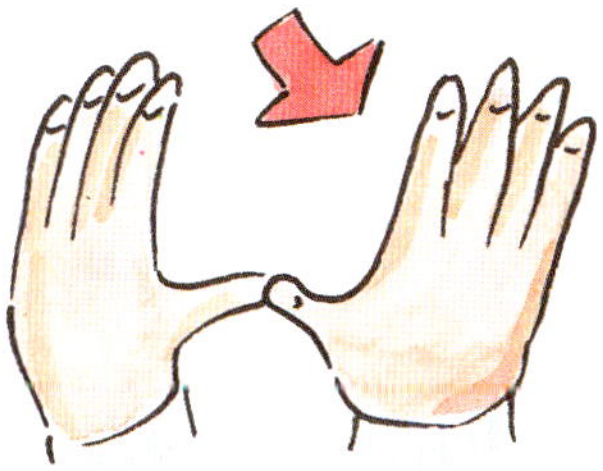

Rooms in a House

cupboard
study
bedroom
living room
hall
porch
basement
utility room

S

sad
This is a sad face.

sailing boat
See Transportation (page 109).

salad
He is making a salad.

salt
She is using too much salt.

same
They look the same.

sand
There is a lot of sand at the beach.

sandwich
It's a gherkin sandwich! Yum!

sandy
The beach is sandy.

Saturday
On Saturday, we work together.

sausage
This dog likes sausages.

saw

A saw is for cutting.

say

She wants to say hello.

scarf

See Clothing (page 25).

school

He learns in school.

scissors

Look what he is cutting with the scissors.

scrub

He wants to scrub the tub.

sea

Whales live in the sea.

seat

The seat is too high.

secret

She is telling a secret.

see

See People (page 77).

seed

When you plant a seed, it grows.

sell

He has many balloons to sell.

send

Mum has to send a letter to her sister.

September

The month after August is September.

seven

See Numbers and Colours (page 68).

seventeen

See Numbers and Colours (page 68).

seventy

See Numbers and Colours (page 69).

shark

A shark has many teeth.

shawl

See Clothing (page 25).

she

She is hiding.

sheep

See Animals (page 11).

shirt

See Clothing (page 24).

shoes

See Clothing (page 25).

shop

He likes to shop.

short

He is too short.

shout

They have to shout.

shovel

She needs a bigger shovel.

show (noun)

They are in a show.

show (verb)

Show us your new tooth!

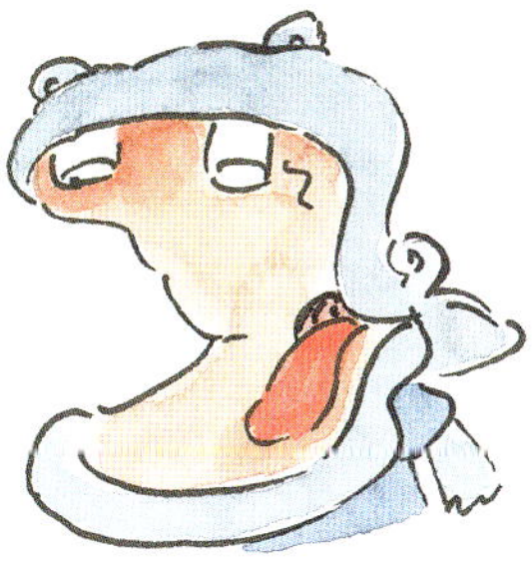

shy

He is very shy.

sick

The rhinoceros is sick.

side

The tree is at the side of the house.

sign

This is the bakery's sign.

S

silly

He has a silly smile.

sing

She loves to sing.

sister

They are sisters.

sit

They want to sit.

six

See Numbers and Colours (page 68).

sixteen

See Numbers and Colours (page 68).

sixty

See Numbers and Colours (page 69).

skateboard

See Transportation (page 108).

skates

See Transportation (page 108).

skating (ice)

See Games and Sports (page 45).

skiing

See Games and Sports (page 45).

skirt

See Clothing (page 25).

sky

The sky is full of stars.

sleep

He is ready to sleep.

slow

A rabbit is quick;
a tortoise is slow.

small

An ant is small.

smell

See People (page 77).

smile

What a big
smile!

smoke

Watch out for
the smoke!

snail

He has a snail
on his nose.

snake

See Animals (page 10).

snore

Try not to
snore.

snow

Snow is white
and cold.

snowball

He is throwing
snowballs.

so

She is so tall!

soap

He is using soap to wash.

socks

See Clothing (page 24).

sofa

The zebras are sitting on the sofa.

some

Some of them are pink.

someday

Dad says I can drive . . . someday.

someone

Someone is behind the fence.

something

Something is under the rug.

song

What song do you think she is singing?

soon

Soon it is going to be noon.

sorry

She is sorry she dropped it.

soup

The soup is hot!

south

It is warm in the south.

special

This is a special car.

spider

This spider is friendly.

spoon

A spoon can't run; can it?

spring

Flowers grow in spring.

square

A square has four sides.

squirrel

There is a squirrel on that hat!

stamp

A stamp goes on a letter.

stand

She does not like to stand.

star

That star is winking.

start

They want to start with A.

stay

He has to stay inside.

step

Try not to step in the puddle.

stick

The dog wants the stick.

sticky

That lollipop is sticky.

stomach

See People (page 76).

stop

You have to stop for a red light.

store

She buys books at the store.

storm
She does not like the storm.

story
We all know this story.

strange
This is a strange animal.

strawberry
This strawberry is big!

street
There is an elephant in the street!

student
The students are all fish.

study
See Rooms in a House (page 87).

suddenly
Suddenly, it is raining.

suit
Something is spilling on his suit.

suitcase
What is in that suitcase?

summer

It is warm in summer.

sun

The sun is hot.

Sunday

On Sunday, we eat dinner with grandma.

sunflower

The sunflower is big and yellow.

sunny

She loves sunny days.

sure

I am sure the door is not going to open.

surprised

She is surprised.

sweets

Sweets are nice.

swim

The fish likes to swim.

swimming

See Games and Sports (page 45).

table

There is a chicken on the table.

table tennis

See Games and Sports (page 44).

tail

He has a long tail.

take

He is going to take the suitcase with him.

talk

They like to talk on the phone.

tall

The red one is very tall.

tambourine

Shake that tambourine!

tan

See Numbers and Colours (page 69).

taste

See People (page 77).

taxi

See Transportation (page 109).

teacher

Our teacher helps us learn.

tear

She has a tear on her cheek.

T

telephone

People can call you on the telephone.

television

My goldfish likes to watch television.

tell

She tells him a story.

ten

See Numbers and Colours (page 68).

tennis

See Games and Sports (page 45).

tent

What is inside the tent?

termite

See Insects (page 53).

terrible

What a terrible mess!

thank

He wants to thank the firefighter.

that

What is that?

their

They are pointing to their suitcases.

them

The shoes belong to them.

then

Get into bed. Then sleep.

there

There she is!

these

No one wants these eggs.

they

See the mice? They are dancing.

thin

One clown is thin.

thing

What is this thing?

think

We use our brain to think.

thirsty

He is thirsty.

thirteen

See Numbers and Colours (page 68).

thirty

See Numbers and Colours (page 69).

this

This baby is sad.

those

Those babies are happy.

thousand

See Numbers and Colours (page 69).

three

See Numbers and Colours (page 68).

through

The ball is coming through the window.

throw

We like to throw the ball.

thumb

See People (page 76).

thunder

Thunder is loud.

Thursday

On Thursday, we wash our clothes.

tie (noun)

See Clothing (page 24).

tie (verb)

He should tie his shoelaces.

tiger

This is a tiger.

time

It is time to wash the dishes.

tired

She is tired.

to

He is going to school.

today

Today is her birthday.

toe

See People (page 77).

together

They are sitting together.

tomato

Mmm! It is a big, juicy tomato.

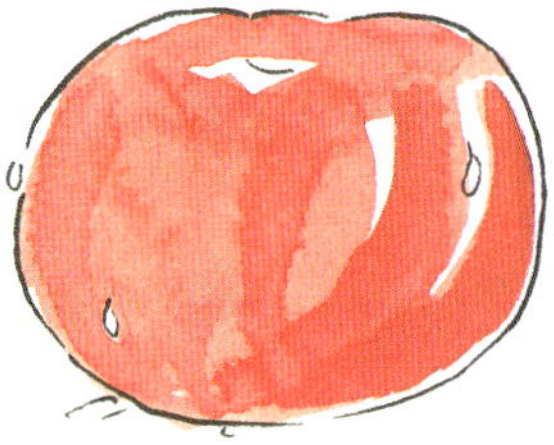

tomorrow

Tomorrow is another day.

tonight

He is sleepy tonight.

too

The baby is singing, too.

tooth

See People (page 77).

toothbrush

My toothbrush is red.

top

The bird is on top.

touch

See People (page 77).

towel

He needs a towel.

town

The ant lives in a town.

toy

He has all kinds of toys.

tracks

These are rabbit tracks.

train

See Transportation (page 108).

trainers

See Clothing (page 25).

treat

A bone is a treat.

tree

There is a cow in that tree.

triangle

A triangle has three sides.

tricks

Her job is to do tricks.

trip (noun)

She is going on a trip.

trip (verb)

The duck tripped.

Transportation

helicopter
sailing boat
car
lorry
boat
underground
horse
taxi
bus

T

trousers

See Clothing (page 24).

trumpet

This is a trumpet.

try

He wants to try to climb it.

Tuesday

On Tuesday we wash the floors.

tulip

There is a tulip on his head.

turn

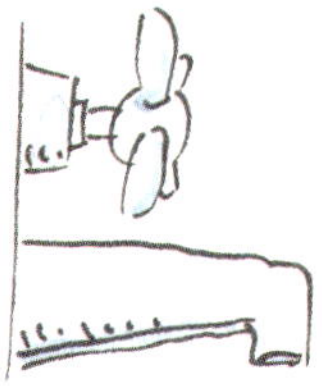

You have to turn the tap.

turtle

That is a fast turtle!

twelve

See Numbers and Colours (page 68).

twenty

See Numbers and Colours (page 68).

twins

They are twins.

two

See Numbers and Colours (page 68).

tyre

One tyre is flat.

ugly

Do you think the toad is ugly?

umbrella

She has a yellow umbrella.

uncle

My uncle is my dad's brother.

under

There is something under the bed.

underground

See Transportation (page 109).

until

He eats until he is full.

up

It is scary up here!

upon

The box is upon the box, upon the box.

upside-down

He is upside-down.

us

Come with us!

use

He needs to use a comb.

utility room

See Rooms in a House (page 87).

V

vacuum cleaner

Here comes the vacuum cleaner!

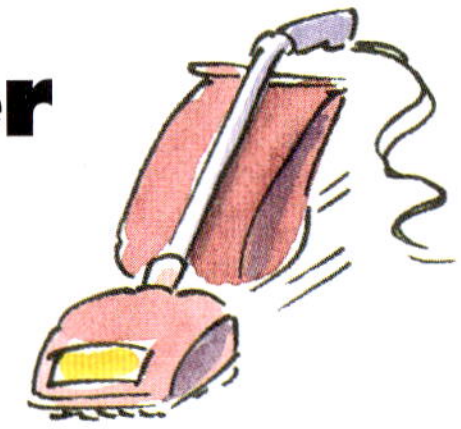

van

See Transportation (page 108).

vegetables

He likes vegetables.

very

It is very cold in there.

vet

A vet helps animals.

village

What a pretty village!

violin

He is playing the violin.

visit

He is going to visit grandma.

volcano

Don't go near the volcano!

waistcoat

See Clothing (page 24).

wait

He has to wait for a bus.

wake up

He is about to wake up.

walk

It is good to walk.

wall

John is building a wall.

warm

It is warm by the fire.

wash

He washes the elephant.

wasp

See Insects (page 52).

watch (noun)

Robert is wearing his new watch.

watch (verb)

Peter watches the ants.

water

The pool is full of water.

we

We are all purple.

weather

What is the weather like today?

Wednesday

On Wednesday, we go to work.

week

Seven days make a week.

welcome

We are always welcome at grandma's house.

well (adverb)

Thomas builds very well.

well (adjective)

She doesn't feel well.

west

The sun goes down in the west.

wet

William is wet.

what

What is outside the window?

wheel

The bicycle needs a new wheel.

when

When you sleep, you close your eyes.

where

This is where he keeps his dinner.

which

Which one do you want?

while

I run while he sleeps.

whiskers

This animal has long whiskers.

whisper

This animal needs to whisper.

whistle

They can hear the whistle.

white

See Numbers and Colours (page 69).

who

Who are you?

whole

Can she eat the whole thing?

why

Why is the baby crying?

wife

She is his wife.

wind

The wind is blowing.

window

I can see through the window.

wink

It is fun to wink.

winter

He skis in the winter.

wish

The girl has a wish.

with

The cat is dancing with the dog.

without

He is going without his sister.

woman

My grandma is a nice woman.

wonderful

They are wonderful dancers.

woods

Someone is walking in the woods.

word

Do not say a word.

work (noun)

That is hard work.

work (verb)

She works very hard.

world

The world is beautiful.

worried

He is worried.

write

Katherine is trying to write with the pencil.

wrong

They are putting on the wrong hats.

X

X-ray
The X-ray shows his bones.

xylophone
He's a great xylophone player.

Y

yawn
What a big yawn!

year
He runs all year.

yellow
See Numbers and Colours (page 69).

yes
Is he yellow?
Yes! He is.

yesterday
Yesterday is the day before today.

you
You are reading this book.

your
What colour are your eyes?

zebra

You cannot have a pet zebra!

zipper

The zipper is stuck.

zigzag

The house has zigzags on it.

zoo

I can see many animals at the zoo.

zip

The bee wants to zip her jacket.

zoom

Rockets zoom into space.

A Family Dinner

Dinner is ready!
It's time to eat.

Here is your
napkin.

The chicken and
vegetables look
delicious.

Please pass the
salt and pepper.

Mmmm! They *are*
delicious!

Dinner is great. Thanks, Mum.
You're welcome, dear.
Do you want more milk?
No, thank you.
May I please be excused?
In a few minutes! But please help us clear the table, first.
Of course.

Meeting and Greeting

Hello!

How are you?

I am fine,
thank you.

Hi!

What is your name?

My name is Maria.
What is your name?

My name is Susan.

What a beautiful day!

Do you live near the park?

Yes, I live across
the street.

Where do you live?

I live in Brown Street.

Do you know what time it is?

It is three o'clock.

Oh, I have to go now.

It was nice to meet you.

Good-bye!

See you soon!

Word List

D

E

F

G

H

Q

R

S